Summary

12.3 Fostering a Future of Hope

8

1

Understanding OCD in Children

1.1 The Basics of Obsessive-Compulsive Disorder

Understanding the fundamentals of Obsessive-Compulsive Disorder (OCD) is crucial for recognizing its impact on children's lives. OCD is a complex mental health condition characterized by a pattern of unwanted thoughts or fears (obsessions) that lead to repetitive behaviors (compulsions). These compulsions are attempts to soothe or counteract the distressing obsessions, creating a cycle that significantly interferes with daily functioning and quality of life.

OCD in children can manifest differently than in adults, with symptoms often misunderstood as mere quirks or typical childhood fears. Early recognition is critical, as it can prevent the escalation of symptoms and facilitate timely intervention. Children may not always understand their experiences or have the language to describe them, making it essential for parents and caregivers to be vigilant about signs that could indicate OCD.

- Obsessions in children might involve excessive concerns about cleanliness, fear of harm coming to themselves or loved ones or an overwhelming need for symmetry and order.

- Compulsions could include washing hands excessively, repeatedly checking things like locks or stoves, arranging objects in a specific manner, and asking for reassurance constantly.

The etiology of OCD involves a combination of genetic, neurological, behavioral, cognitive, and environmental factors. Research suggests that changes in the body's natural chemistry or brain functions might play a role. Additionally, children who have experienced trauma or significant stress may be more susceptible to developing OCD.

Treatment approaches for OCD typically involve cognitive-behavioral therapy (CBT), particularly Exposure and Response Prevention (ERP), which has been shown to be effective for many children. In some cases, medication may also be recommended to manage symptoms. It's important for treatment plans to be tailored individually, taking into consideration the child's age, specific symptoms, and any other co-existing conditions.

Creating a supportive environment at home and school is vital for children struggling with OCD. This includes educating family members and educators about the disorder to foster understanding and empathy. Encouraging open communication allows children to express their feelings without fear of judgment or dismissal.

In conclusion, while OCD can present significant challenges for affected children and their families, understanding its basics lays the groundwork for compassionate support and effective management strategies. With appropriate care and intervention, children with OCD can lead fulfilling lives despite their condition.

1.2 Differentiating Between Normal Worries and OCD

Understanding the distinction between typical childhood worries and Obsessive-Compulsive Disorder (OCD) is crucial for early identification and intervention. While it's normal for children to experience fears and anxieties as they navigate through various developmental stages, OCD represents a more severe spectrum of anxiety disorders characterized by persistent, intrusive thoughts (obsessions) and repetitive behaviors (compulsions).

Normal worries in children are usually transient and vary according to their age and developmental stage. For instance, young children might fear the dark or imaginary creatures, whereas older children may worry about school performance or peer relationships. These concerns are generally proportional to real-life situations and tend to resolve with reassurance and coping strategies.

In contrast, OCD in children manifests as excessive and irrational worries that lead to compulsive behaviors aimed at alleviating the distress caused by these obsessions. For example, a child with OCD might fear germs to an extreme extent, leading them to wash their hands repetitively until they're raw. Unlike normal worries, these obsessions and compulsions are time-consuming, significantly interfere with daily functioning, and do not alleviate despite logical reasoning or reassurance from others.

- Normal worries are often related to specific events or situations and diminish once the event passes or the situation is resolved.

- OCD-related fears are pervasive, persistent, and can escalate over time without appropriate intervention.

- While typical childhood fears can be assuaged with comfort from caregivers, OCD compulsions require more structured interventions such as cognitive-behavioral therapy (CBT).

Differentiating between normal worries and OCD involves observing the intensity, duration, and impact of the child's fears on their daily life. A key indicator of OCD is when the child engages in rituals or behaviors that they feel driven to perform despite them being logically unnecessary or when these actions consume significant amounts of time daily.

Early recognition of these signs is essential for providing timely support. Parents noticing persistent patterns of excessive worry accompanied by ritualistic behavior should consider seeking a professional evaluation. Understanding this distinction not only aids in early diagnosis but also in preventing potential escalation of symptoms, paving the way for effective management strategies tailored specifically for children with OCD.

1.3 Recognizing the Signs and Symptoms in Kids

Identifying the signs and symptoms of Obsessive-Compulsive Disorder (OCD) in children is a critical step towards understanding and managing this condition effectively. Unlike adults, who can articulate their feelings and fears more clearly, children may not always be able to express what they are experiencing internally. This makes recognizing the external manifestations of OCD in kids an essential skill for parents, caregivers, and educators.

OCD in children often presents through a combination of obsessionsâ€"unwanted and distressing thoughts or images that repeatedly enter the mindâ€"and compulsions, which are behaviors or rituals performed to try to alleviate the anxiety caused by these obsessions. Recognizing these patterns requires careful observation and understanding of how they diverge from typical childhood behaviors.

- Excessive Worry Over Contamination: One common sign is an irrational fear of germs or dirt, leading to excessive handwashing, avoiding touching certain objects, or extreme cleanliness that goes beyond typical concerns about hygiene.

- Repetitive Behaviors: Engaging in rituals like counting, tapping, touching objects a specific number of times before feeling safe to proceed with an activity, or insisting on routines being performed in an exact manner without deviation.

- Intrusive Thoughts: Children may express fear of harm coming to themselves or loved ones despite no real threat. They might seek constant reassurance from adults about these fears.

- Avoidance: Avoiding places, situations, or people that trigger their obsessions. For example, a child might refuse to go to school for fear of contamination or avoid social situations because they involve unpredictability that could disrupt their compulsive routines.

Distinguishing between normal childhood fears and those stemming from OCD involves noting the intensity, frequency, and impact of these behaviors on the child's life. While it's common for children to have routines or specific likes and dislikes, those with OCD feel driven by their rituals; they experience significant distress if unable to perform them. These behaviors are time-consumingâ€"often taking up more than 1 hour per dayâ€"and interfere with social interactions, school performance, and daily activities.

Early recognition and intervention are key. If you notice persistent patterns that align with OCD symptomsâ€"especially if they cause distress or functional impairmentâ€"it's important to seek a professional evaluation. Understanding these signs not only aids in early diagnosis but also opens pathways for effective treatment strategies tailored specifically for children.

References:

- American Psychiatric Association. (2013). Diagnostic and Statistical Manual of Mental Disorders (5th ed.). Arlington, VA: American Psychiatric Publishing.

- March, J.S., & Benton, C.M. (2007). Practical considerations in the treatment of children with obsessive-compulsive disorder. Pediatric Drugs, 9(6), 391-401.

- Rapoport, J.L., & Inoff-Germain, G. (2000). Treatment of obsessive-compulsive disorder in children and adolescents. Journal of Child Psychology and Psychiatry, 41(4), 419-431.

- Storch, E.A., Murphy, T.K., Geffken, G.R., Sajid, M., Allen, P., Roberti, J.W., & Goodman, W.K. (2004). Psychometric evaluation of the Children's Yale-Brown Obsessive Compulsive Scale. Psychiatry Research, 129(1), 91-98.

2

The Impact of OCD on Childhood Development

2.1 Emotional and Psychological Effects

The emotional and psychological ramifications of Obsessive-Compulsive Disorder (OCD) in children are profound, influencing not only the child's mental health but also their social development and overall quality of life. Understanding these effects is crucial for parents, caregivers, and educators to provide the necessary support and interventions.

OCD can manifest in a child's life through a variety of symptoms, including recurrent, unwanted thoughts (obsessions) and repetitive behaviors (compulsions) that they feel driven to perform. These symptoms can lead to significant emotional distress for the child. They may experience feelings of anxiety or fear over seemingly minor issues to others but feel insurmountable to them due to their OCD.

Children with OCD often struggle with feelings of shame or embarrassment about their thoughts or behaviors, which can lead to social withdrawal or isolation. They might fear judgment from peers if their compulsions or obsessions are noticed, impacting their ability to form healthy relationships. This isolation can exacerbate feelings of loneliness and misunderstanding, further affecting their emotional well-being.

The constant battle with their own thoughts can be exhausting for children with OCD, leading to increased irritability or mood swings. The stress of managing OCD on top of regular childhood challenges can result in heightened sensitivity to stressful situations, making it difficult for them to cope with normal daily stresses.

- Anxiety and fear tied directly to obsessions or compulsions

- Shame or embarrassment about their symptoms leading to social withdrawal

- Irritability or mood swings due to the mental exhaustion from battling OCD

- Increased sensitivity to stress, complicating typical childhood experiences

In addition to these direct emotional impacts, children with OCD may also face psychological effects such as low self-esteem and a persistent sense of inadequacy. The relentless nature of OCD can make children feel different from their peers, fostering a negative self-image that affects how they view themselves within various contextsâ€"academically, socially, and at home.

It is essential for those supporting children with OCDâ€"whether family members, educators, or healthcare professionalsâ€"to recognize these emotional and psychological effects. By understanding the depth of impact beyond just the visible symptoms, caregivers can tailor support strategies that address both the behavioral aspects of OCD as well as its profound emotional toll on children's lives.

2.2 Social Implications and Peer Relationships

The social landscape of childhood is complex, filled with learning experiences that shape a child's development and self-perception. For children with Obsessive-Compulsive Disorder (OCD), navigating this landscape can be particularly challenging. The impact of OCD on peer relationships and social interactions is profound, influencing not only the child's ability to form friendships but also their overall social development.

Children with OCD often experience difficulties in engaging with peers due to the time-consuming nature of their compulsions or the fear of their obsessions being exposed. This can lead to missed social opportunities, as they may avoid situations where their OCD symptoms could be triggered or noticed. For example, a child who has compulsions related to cleanliness might avoid birthday parties or outdoor activities, which are critical for peer bonding at a young age.

Beyond the avoidance of social situations, children with OCD may also face direct stigma or misunderstanding from their peers. Children are naturally curious and sometimes lack the filter that comes with maturity; thus, they might ask questions or make comments that feel invasive or judgmental to someone with OCD. This can exacerbate feelings of isolation and difference, reinforcing the childâ€™s sense of being 'other' or not fitting in.

The strain on peer relationships extends into group dynamics within educational settings as well. Group projects and collaborative classroom activities require flexibility and adaptabilityâ€"traits that children struggling with OCD might find challenging to exhibit due to their need for control or fear of contamination. This can lead to frustration among peers who may not understand why their classmate is behaving differently, potentially leading to exclusion or bullying.

- Difficulty engaging in typical childhood activities due to avoidance behaviors

- Misunderstanding and stigma from peers leading to social isolation

- Challenges in group dynamics within educational settings

- Potential for exclusion or bullying due to misunderstood behaviors

In light of these challenges, it is crucial for parents, educators, and caregivers to foster an environment of understanding and acceptance around children with OCD. Educating peers about the disorder, encouraging inclusive behavior, and providing structured opportunities for positive social interactions can mitigate some of the negative impacts on peer relationships. By addressing these issues proactively, adults can help children with OCD build meaningful connections with others while navigating the complexities of their condition.

2.3 Academic Challenges and Support Strategies

The academic journey is a critical component of childhood development, offering not just education but also opportunities for social interaction, personal growth, and the acquisition of life skills. For children with Obsessive-Compulsive Disorder (OCD), however, this path can be fraught with unique challenges that impact their learning experience and overall school performance. Understanding these challenges is the first step towards implementing effective support strategies that can help these students thrive academically.

Children with OCD may face significant obstacles in maintaining concentration and completing tasks within set timeframes due to intrusive thoughts or compulsive behaviors. For instance, a student might feel compelled to organize their desk meticulously before they can start an assignment, significantly cutting into their work time. Additionally, the fear of contamination could deter them from participating in hands-on activities or using shared resources like computer keyboards or laboratory equipment.

Moreover, the social difficulties stemming from OCD, as discussed in the previous section on social implications and peer relationships, can extend into academic settings. These issues can lead to further isolation within the classroom environment and hinder group learning experiences. The stigma or misunderstanding from peers about a child's compulsions or avoidance behaviors can exacerbate feelings of anxiety and depression, which in turn negatively affects academic motivation and engagement.

- Disruptions in concentration due to intrusive thoughts or compulsions

- Avoidance of certain activities or resources due to fear of contamination

- Social isolation impacting group learning experiences

- Negative effects on motivation and engagement stemming from anxiety and depression

To address these academic challenges effectively, schools and educators need to adopt tailored support strategies that accommodate the needs of students with OCD. Creating a flexible learning environment where adjustments can be made to deadlines or task formats is crucial. For example, allowing extra time for assignments or providing alternative ways to complete tasks that trigger OCD symptoms can make a significant difference in a student's ability to participate fully in their education.

Furthermore, fostering an inclusive classroom culture that promotes understanding and acceptance among peers is essential. Educators should consider incorporating lessons on mental health awareness into the curriculum to reduce stigma and encourage empathy towards students with OCD. Providing training for teachers on how to recognize and respond appropriately to the signs of OCD can also ensure timely support for affected students.

In conclusion, while children with OCD face distinct academic challenges, thoughtful implementation of support strategies by educators and caregivers can mitigate these obstacles. By creating an accommodating educational environment that addresses both academic needs and emotional well-being, we empower students with OCD to achieve their full potential.

References:

- American Psychiatric Association. (2013). Diagnostic and Statistical Manual of Mental Disorders (5th ed.). Arlington, VA: American Psychiatric Publishing.

- Piacentini, J., & Langley, A. (2004). Cognitive-behavioral therapy for children with obsessive-compulsive disorder: Patient and family guide. Los Angeles, CA: UCLA Child OCD, Anxiety, and Tic Disorders Program.

- Storch, E.A., & Murphy, T.K. (Eds.). (2014). Handbook of Child and Adolescent Obsessive-Compulsive Disorder. Lawrence Erlbaum Associates Publishers.

- March, J.S., & Mulle, K. (1998). OCD in Children and Adolescents: A Cognitive-Behavioral Treatment Manual. New York: Guilford Press.

3

Early Detection and Diagnosis

3.1 Identifying Early Warning Signs

The identification of early warning signs in children with Obsessive-Compulsive Disorder (OCD) is a critical step towards timely intervention and support. Recognizing these signs not only aids in the early diagnosis but also in the implementation of effective treatment strategies. This section delves into the nuances of identifying these early indicators, offering insights into the subtle yet significant shifts in behavior and emotional state that may signal the onset of OCD in children.

OCD manifests through a variety of symptoms, which can often be mistaken for typical childhood behaviors or dismissed as phases that children will outgrow. However, distinguishing between normal developmental behaviors and potential early signs of

OCD is essential. These signs include excessive handwashing, repeated checking of locks or appliances, an overwhelming need for order and symmetry, and persistent fears or thoughts that lead to specific compulsions or rituals. Unlike typical routines or habits, these behaviors are driven by intense anxiety or distress.

- Excessive concern with cleanliness or contamination beyond age-appropriate curiosity.

- Repetitive behaviors or rituals that the child feels compelled to perform, even if they recognize them as unnecessary.

- Extreme distress when prevented from performing these rituals.

- An unusual preoccupation with order, symmetry, or exactness in a manner that interferes with daily activities.

- Persistent and intrusive thoughts that are distressing to the child.

In addition to behavioral indicators, emotional signs are equally telling. Children may exhibit increased irritability, frustration, or moodiness stemming from their inability to control their thoughts or compulsions. They might also show signs of withdrawal from social interactions due to fear of judgment or misunderstanding by peers. It's crucial for parents, caregivers, and educators to approach these observations with sensitivity and understanding rather than dismissal.

Early detection involves a keen observation of changes in behavior patterns over time. It requires patience and open communication between children and adults. Encouraging children to express their feelings and fears without fear of reprimand plays a pivotal role in identifying OCD symptoms early on. By fostering an environment where children feel safe sharing their experiences, adults can better discern between typical developmental stages and potential warning signs of OCD.

This nuanced understanding underscores the importance of vigilance and empathy in recognizing early warning signs of OCD in children. It highlights how proactive observation combined with compassionate engagement can facilitate timely interventionâ€"laying a foundation for effective management and support for young individuals navigating the challenges posed by this disorder.

3.2 Navigating the Diagnosis Process with Professionals

The journey towards obtaining a diagnosis for Obsessive-Compulsive Disorder (OCD) in children can be complex and emotionally taxing for families. Understanding how to effectively navigate this process with healthcare professionals is crucial for securing the support and treatment necessary for managing the disorder. This section explores the steps involved in the diagnostic process, highlighting the importance of collaboration between families and professionals.

Initially, recognizing the need to seek professional help often stems from observing persistent behaviors or emotional distress in a child that aligns with OCD symptoms. Once these concerns are identified, the next step involves consulting with a primary care physician or pediatrician who can provide preliminary assessments and referrals to specialists in mental health, such as psychologists or psychiatrists experienced in treating OCD.

Engaging with these specialists is a critical phase where detailed evaluations are conducted through clinical interviews, behavioral observations, and sometimes standardized assessment tools. These evaluations aim to understand the severity and impact of symptoms on the child's functioning. Families play an essential role during this stage by providing comprehensive insights into their child's behavior patterns, emotional states, and any changes observed over time.

- Preparation for appointments by gathering information on symptom history and family medical background.

- Active participation in discussions during evaluations to ensure all relevant information is shared.

- Asking questions about diagnosis criteria, treatment options, and expected outcomes to make informed decisions.

Beyond initial diagnosis, establishing a collaborative relationship with healthcare providers is vital for ongoing management of OCD. This includes regular follow-ups to monitor progress, adjustments in treatment plans as needed, and discussions about any new challenges that arise. Effective communication between families and professionals not only facilitates better outcomes but also empowers parents and caregivers in supporting their child's journey towards recovery.

In conclusion, navigating the diagnosis process requires patience, persistence, and proactive engagement from both families and healthcare professionals. By understanding each step of this journey and participating actively in it, families can advocate for their child's needs effectively—laying a strong foundation for successful management of OCD.

3.3 Understanding Medical Assessments and Their Importance

The process of medical assessments in the diagnosis and management of Obsessive-Compulsive Disorder (OCD) in children is a critical step that requires careful consideration and understanding. These assessments serve as the foundation for developing an effective treatment plan tailored to the child's specific needs. This section delves into the intricacies of medical assessments, emphasizing their significance in ensuring accurate diagnosis and facilitating optimal care.

Medical assessments for OCD typically involve a comprehensive evaluation that includes clinical interviews, behavioral observations, and the use of standardized assessment tools. The primary aim is to gather detailed information about the child's symptoms, including their nature, frequency, severity, and impact on daily functioning. This multifaceted approach helps healthcare professionals distinguish OCD symptoms from those of other mental health disorders, which is crucial for accurate diagnosis.

One key aspect of these assessments is the clinical interview, which allows specialists to obtain a thorough history of the child's behavior and emotional state directly from the child and their family members. This narrative can reveal patterns that are essential for understanding the disorder's impact on the child's life. Additionally, behavioral observations during these interviews provide real-time insights into how OCD manifests in various settings.

- Utilization of standardized assessment tools to quantify symptom severity and track changes over time.

- Inclusion of family members in discussions to gain a holistic view of the childâ€™s condition.

- Evaluation of co-occurring conditions that may influence treatment planning.

Beyond diagnosis, medical assessments play a pivotal role in ongoing management by enabling healthcare providers to monitor progress and adjust treatment plans as necessary. Regular reassessment ensures that interventions remain aligned with the childâ€™s evolving needs, thereby maximizing therapeutic outcomes. Furthermore, these evaluations facilitate communication between families and healthcare professionals by providing objective data that can guide discussions about treatment expectations and goals.

In conclusion, understanding medical assessments' scope and significance is paramount for families navigating OCD management. By actively participating in this process and collaborating with healthcare professionals, families can advocate more effectively for their childâ€™s needsâ€"laying a solid foundation for successful intervention strategies.

References:

- American Psychiatric Association. (2013). Diagnostic and statistical manual of mental disorders (5th ed.). Arlington, VA: American Psychiatric Publishing.

- Storch, E. A., Lewin, A. B., De Nadai, A. S., & Murphy, T. K. (2010). Clinical Handbook of Obsessive-Compulsive Disorder and Related Problems. Baltimore, MD: Johns Hopkins University Press.

- Piacentini, J., Bergman, R. L., Keller, M., & McCracken, J. (2003). Functional impairment in children and adolescents with obsessive-compulsive disorder. Journal of Child and Adolescent Psychopharmacology, 13(Suppl 1), S61-S69.

- Foa, E.B., Coles, M., Huppert, J.D., Pasupuleti, R.V., Franklin, M.E., & March, J.S. (2010). Development and validation of a child version of the Obsessive Compulsive Inventory. Behavior Therapy, 41(1), 121-132.

4

Treatment Options for Childhood OCD

4.1 Cognitive-Behavioral Therapy (CBT) Techniques for Kids

The significance of Cognitive-Behavioral Therapy (CBT) in treating Obsessive-Compulsive Disorder (OCD) in children cannot be overstated. This therapeutic approach is tailored to help kids understand the connection between their thoughts, feelings, and behaviors, which is crucial in managing OCD symptoms. CBT techniques are designed to empower children, giving them the tools to challenge and overcome the intrusive thoughts and compulsive behaviors characteristic of OCD.

One core component of CBT for children with OCD is Exposure and Response Prevention (ERP). This technique involves gradually exposing the child to situations or objects that trigger their OCD symptoms, without allowing them to perform their usual compulsive responses. Over time, ERP helps reduce the anxiety associated with these triggers, teaching kids that they can manage their fear without resorting to compulsive behavior.

- Cognitive Restructuring: This technique helps children identify and challenge irrational beliefs that fuel their OCD symptoms. By learning to recognize these thought patterns, kids can start to replace them with more realistic and balanced perspectives.

- Relaxation Training: Children are taught various relaxation techniques such as deep breathing exercises or progressive muscle relaxation. These methods can help lower overall anxiety levels, making it easier for them to engage in ERP and other CBT strategies.

- Social Skills Training: Given that OCD can significantly impact a child's social interactions, this aspect of CBT focuses on improving communication skills, assertiveness, and problem-solving abilities within social contexts.

Incorporating family involvement is another critical aspect of CBT for kids with OCD. Parents and caregivers are educated on how best to support their child through treatment without inadvertently reinforcing their OCD behaviors. This collaborative approach ensures that the child feels supported both within therapy sessions and at home.

Moreover, technology-assisted CBT programs have emerged as valuable tools in delivering therapy more flexibly. Through apps or online platforms offering guided CBT sessions, children can engage with therapeutic exercises outside traditional settings under parental supervision or as part of a therapist-guided plan.

In conclusion, CBT offers a comprehensive framework for helping children with OCD confront their fears directly while equipping them with lifelong skills for managing anxiety. By focusing on changing thought patterns and behaviors through structured techniques like ERP, cognitive restructuring, relaxation training, social skills development, and leveraging technology-assisted programsâ€"CBT stands out as an effective treatment modality tailored specifically for young individuals navigating the challenges of OCD.

4.2 Medication Management Tips

The management of medication for children with Obsessive-Compulsive Disorder (OCD) is a critical component of their overall treatment plan. While Cognitive-Behavioral Therapy (CBT) offers significant benefits, certain cases necessitate the inclusion of pharmacotherapy to effectively manage symptoms. Understanding how to navigate medication management can significantly enhance the treatment outcomes for children with OCD.

Firstly, it's essential to recognize that the decision to initiate medication should be made collaboratively between healthcare providers, parents, and when appropriate, the child. This inclusive approach ensures that all parties are informed and comfortable with the treatment strategy. Selective Serotonin Reuptake Inhibitors (SSRIs) are commonly prescribed for childhood OCD due to their efficacy and relatively favorable side effect profile compared to other psychotropic medications.

When managing medication for OCD, starting with a low dose and gradually increasing based on response and tolerability is a prudent strategy. This "start low, go slow" approach helps minimize side effects, which can be particularly concerning in pediatric populations. Regular monitoring by a healthcare provider is crucial during this titration phase to adjust dosages as needed and address any concerns that arise.

- Open Communication: Encourage open dialogue between the child, parents, and healthcare providers about the medication's effects, including any side effects or changes in symptoms. This communication is vital for adjusting treatment plans promptly.

- Educational Support: Parents and children should be educated about the expected timeline for improvement with SSRIs, which often takes several weeks before significant benefits are observed. Setting realistic expectations can help maintain adherence to the medication regimen.

- Lifestyle Considerations: Discussing lifestyle factors such as diet, exercise, and sleep hygiene can complement pharmacotherapy. For instance, maintaining a regular sleep schedule may enhance the effectiveness of medication and improve overall well-being.

In addition to these strategies, it's important for families to have access to resources such as support groups or educational materials specifically geared towards pediatric OCD. These resources can provide additional coping strategies and reduce feelings of isolation by connecting families experiencing similar challenges.

In conclusion, effective medication management for childhood OCD involves a combination of careful planning, ongoing communication among all stakeholders involved in care delivery (including the child), education on what to expect from pharmacotherapy, attention to lifestyle factors that could influence treatment outcomes, and leveraging available support resources. By adopting these comprehensive approaches within a framework of informed consent and collaboration, children with OCD can achieve optimal results from their medication regimen alongside other therapeutic interventions like CBT.

4.3 Exploring Holistic Approaches and Mindfulness Exercises

The exploration of holistic approaches and mindfulness exercises represents a significant shift towards integrating complementary therapies in the treatment of childhood OCD. This approach underscores the importance of viewing the child as a whole rather than focusing solely on symptom management. Holistic methods, including mindfulness, aim to enhance overall well-being, reduce stress levels, and improve coping mechanisms, thereby indirectly addressing OCD symptoms.

Mindfulness exercises are particularly beneficial as they teach children how to focus on the present moment in a non-judgmental manner. This skill can be incredibly useful for managing the intrusive thoughts and compulsive behaviors characteristic of OCD. By learning to observe their thoughts without engaging or reacting to them automatically, children can gain greater control over their responses to these thoughts.

- Introduction to Mindfulness: Starting with simple breathing exercises can help introduce children to mindfulness practices. Techniques such as "belly breathing" or "mindful coloring" are accessible ways for children to learn about being present.

- Yoga for Children: Yoga combines physical activity with mindfulness, making it an excellent holistic approach for managing anxiety and stress related to OCD. The practice encourages body awareness, relaxation, and mental focus.

- Nature Therapy: Spending time in nature has been shown to reduce stress and improve mood. Activities like walking in a park or gardening can serve as therapeutic exercises that promote mindfulness and connection with the environment.

In addition to these practices, incorporating holistic dietary considerations can also play a role in managing OCD symptoms. While no specific diet cures OCD, ensuring that children consume balanced meals rich in nutrients can support overall brain health and emotional regulation. Omega-3 fatty acids, found in fish and flaxseeds, for example, have been linked to improved mental health outcomes.

It's important for parents and caregivers considering holistic approaches and mindfulness exercises for their child's OCD treatment plan to consult with healthcare professionals. This ensures that these complementary therapies are appropriately integrated with conventional treatments like CBT and medication management when necessary. By adopting a comprehensive treatment strategy that includes holistic methods, children with OCD can achieve better outcomes through enhanced resilience, reduced anxiety levels, and improved quality of life.

References:

- Zylowska, L. et al. (2008). Mindfulness Meditation Training in Adults and Adolescents With ADHD: A Feasibility Study. Journal of Attention Disorders.

- Kabat-Zinn, J. (1994). Wherever You Go, There You Are: Mindfulness Meditation in Everyday Life. Hyperion.

- Hofmann, S.G., Sawyer, A.T., Witt, A.A., & Oh, D. (2010). The effect of mindfulness-based therapy on anxiety and depression: A meta-analytic review. Journal of Consulting and Clinical Psychology.

- Greeson, J.M. (2009). Mindfulness Research Update: 2008.Complementary Health Practice Review.

- Biegel, G.M., Brown, K.W., Shapiro, S.L., & Schubert, C.M. (2009). Mindfulness-Based Stress Reduction for the Treatment of Adolescent Psychiatric Outpatients: A Randomized Clinical Trial. Journal of Consulting and Clinical Psychology.

5

Creating a Supportive Environment at Home

5.1 Encouraging Open Communication

The cornerstone of creating a supportive environment for children with OCD is fostering an atmosphere where open communication is not just encouraged but nurtured. This chapter delves into the critical role that open dialogue plays in understanding and managing OCD within the family dynamic. It's about building bridges of empathy, trust, and understanding between parents or caregivers and their children.

Open communication goes beyond merely talking about day-to-day activities; it involves creating a safe space where children feel comfortable sharing their fears, anxieties, and the intricacies of their experiences with OCD without fear of judgment or reprimand. This level of openness allows parents to gain insights into the triggers and manifestations of their child's OCD, facilitating more effective support and intervention strategies.

- Establishing regular check-ins: Designating specific times for open-ended conversations can help normalize discussing feelings and challenges related to OCD.

- Active listening: Showing genuine interest in what the child has to say, acknowledging their feelings without immediate correction or advice-giving encourages more frequent sharing.

- Educational dialogues: Integrating discussions about OCD within everyday conversations helps demystify the disorder, making it a less daunting topic for both the child and family members.

In addition to these strategies, it's crucial for parents to model open communication themselves. Sharing oneâ€™s own feelings and thoughts about challenges (in an age-appropriate manner) can demonstrate that vulnerability is not only acceptable but valued. This mutual exchange fosters a deeper connection and reinforces that no subject is too taboo or frightening to discuss openly at home.

Moreover, encouraging open communication extends beyond verbal exchanges. It includes non-verbal cues such as body language and emotional reactions. Parents should be mindful of how their responsesâ€"whether verbal or non-verbalâ€"might either encourage or inhibit further sharing from their child. For instance, maintaining eye contact, nodding in understanding, or offering a comforting gesture can significantly enhance communicative effectiveness.

In essence, encouraging open communication forms the bedrock upon which other supportive strategies are built. It not only aids in managing OCD symptoms more effectively but also strengthens the familial bonds through shared experiences and mutual support. By prioritizing this approach, families can navigate the complexities of OCD with greater resilience, understanding, and hope for overcoming the challenges together.

5.2 Building Routines that Accommodate Your Childâ€™s Needs

The establishment of routines is a fundamental aspect of creating a supportive environment for children with OCD. These routines not only provide a sense of structure and predictability, which can be particularly comforting for children dealing with anxiety and compulsions, but they also ensure that the child's specific needs are met in a consistent manner. Tailoring these routines to accommodate your child's unique requirements can significantly enhance their ability to manage symptoms and engage in daily activities more effectively.

Routines centered around your childâ€™s needs might include specific morning rituals that help ease the transition from home to school, or evening routines that promote relaxation and readiness for sleep. The key is flexibility within the structure; while maintaining a general framework, parents should be prepared to adjust routines as needed based on their childâ€™s day-to-day experiences and challenges with OCD.

- Creating a visual schedule: Using charts or boards to visually map out daily or weekly routines can help children understand what to expect, reducing anxiety about the unknown.

- Incorporating time for OCD management: Designating periods within the routine for practices such as mindfulness exercises or therapy homework can normalize these activities and reinforce their importance.

- Building in choice: Allowing children some degree of choice within their routine (e.g., selecting an outfit or choosing between two pre-approved breakfast options) can foster a sense of autonomy and control.

Beyond the practical aspects of managing OCD symptoms, these personalized routines play a crucial role in strengthening the parent-child relationship. They demonstrate to the child that their feelings and experiences are valid and important, reinforcing the open communication established as foundational in fostering a supportive environment. Moreover, by actively involving children in the creation and adjustment of their routines, parents empower them to take an active role in managing their condition, promoting resilience and self-efficacy.

It's also essential for parents to model adaptability by showing how adjustments can be made when routines are disrupted. This teaches children that while consistency is helpful, it's equally important to be able to adapt to changesâ€"a valuable lesson not just for managing OCD but for life in general. Through thoughtful construction of daily routines that respect both the need for structure and flexibility, families can create a nurturing environment where children with OCD feel supported in every aspect of their lives.

5.3 Fostering Independence While Providing Necessary Support

The delicate balance between fostering independence and providing the necessary support for children with OCD is a critical aspect of creating a supportive home environment. This approach empowers children to manage their symptoms effectively while ensuring they do not feel alone in their struggles. The goal is to build their confidence and self-reliance, equipping them with the tools they need to face challenges head-on, both now and in the future.

Encouraging independence in children with OCD involves teaching them problem-solving skills that they can apply when facing obsessions or compulsions. This might include cognitive-behavioral strategies learned in therapy, such as exposure and response prevention (ERP) techniques, which they can initiate on their own when appropriate. However, it's crucial that parents remain available to provide guidance and reassurance as needed, stepping back gradually as the child demonstrates readiness to handle more on their own.

- Setting realistic goals: Begin with small, achievable tasks that the child can accomplish independently, gradually increasing complexity as their confidence grows.

- Offering choices: Empower children by allowing them to make decisions about their daily activities or how they wish to tackle their OCD management practices.

- Providing tools and resources: Equip children with resources such as books, apps, or access to online communities where they can learn more about managing OCD independently.

This strategy does not mean leaving children to navigate their condition alone; rather, it's about being a supportive presence that encourages autonomy while being ready to step in when necessary. For instance, parents might discuss potential strategies with their child after an anxiety-provoking situation has passed rather than taking control during the event. This approach helps the child reflect on what they could do differently next time, reinforcing learning through experience.

In essence, fostering independence while providing necessary support requires a nuanced understanding of each child's unique needs and capabilities. It involves encouraging them to take ownership of their journey through OCD management while ensuring they know support is always available. By striking this balance, parents can help their children build resilience and develop a sense of mastery over their symptomsâ€"a foundation that will serve them well throughout life.

References:

- American Psychiatric Association. (2013). Diagnostic and Statistical Manual of Mental Disorders (5th ed.). Arlington, VA: American Psychiatric Publishing.

- March, J.S., & Benton, C.M. (2007). Talking Back to OCD: The Program That Helps Kids and Teens Say "No Way" -- and Parents Say "Way to Go". New York: Guilford Press.

- Storch, E.A., & Lewin, A.B. (Eds.). (2011). Handbook of Child and Adolescent Obsessive-Compulsive Disorder. New York: Routledge.

- Anxiety and Depression Association of America. (n.d.). Childhood OCD. Retrieved from https://adaa.org/understanding-anxiety/obsessive-compulsive-disorder-ocd/childhood-ocd

- International OCD Foundation. (n.d.). What is Cognitive Behavioral Therapy? Retrieved from https://iocdf.org/about-ocd/ocd-treatment/cbt/

6

Managing School Life

6.1 Advocating for Your Child’s Needs in Educational Settings

The journey of advocating for a child with OCD within educational settings is both crucial and challenging. It involves navigating a complex landscape of policies, understanding individual rights, and fostering partnerships with educators. This process is vital to ensure that children receive the support and accommodations they need to thrive academically and socially.

Advocacy begins with knowledge. Parents and caregivers must familiarize themselves with the legal frameworks that protect their child's educational rights, such as the Individuals with Disabilities Education Act (IDEA) in the United States. Understanding these laws provides a foundation upon which to build an effective advocacy strategy.

Communication is another cornerstone of successful advocacy. Establishing open, collaborative relationships with teachers, school counselors, and administrators can facilitate the development of tailored support plans. It's important for parents to share insights into their child's needs, triggers, and effective coping strategies, ensuring that school staff are well-equipped to provide appropriate support.

- Documenting everything is essential for accountability and progress tracking. Keeping detailed records of meetings, correspondence, and educational plans helps safeguard a child's right to appropriate accommodations.

- Seeking allies within the school community can amplify advocacy efforts. This might include connecting with special education teachers or school psychologists who understand OCD's impact on learning and can advocate from within the system.

- Exploring external support services such as tutoring or therapy outside school hours can complement school-based interventions, offering additional avenues for managing OCD symptoms effectively.

In addition to these practical steps, it's important for parents to cultivate resilience and patience. Change within educational systems can be slow, and advocating for a child's needs often requires persistence. Celebrating small victories along the way can help maintain momentum and remind all involved of the ultimate goal: supporting a child's ability to learn and grow despite OCD.

Ultimately, advocating for a child with OCD in educational settings is about more than securing accommodations; it's about fostering understanding and empathy among educators and peers alike. By taking proactive steps to advocate effectively, parents can help create an inclusive environment where children with OCD are empowered to achieve their full potential.

6.2 Collaborating with Teachers and School Counselors

The partnership between parents, teachers, and school counselors is pivotal in creating a supportive educational environment for children, especially those with specific needs such as OCD. This collaboration goes beyond mere communication; it involves active engagement and shared responsibility in the child's academic and social development. Understanding the roles each party plays can significantly enhance the effectiveness of this collaboration.

Teachers are on the front lines of a child's daily school experience. They observe behaviors, identify challenges, and provide the immediate educational support necessary for learning. However, their role extends further when they collaborate closely with parents and counselors. By sharing observations about a child's progress, struggles, or changes in behavior, teachers can offer invaluable insights that contribute to tailored support strategies.

School counselors play a crucial intermediary role. They possess expertise in both educational processes and psychological well-being, making them essential allies in addressing a child's needs holistically. Counselors can facilitate discussions between parents and teachers, ensuring that all parties have a clear understanding of the child's needs and how best to meet them within the school setting.

- Developing Individualized Education Plans (IEPs) or 504 plans that outline specific accommodations or interventions needed for the child to succeed.

- Organizing regular meetings to discuss the child's progress and adjust strategies as necessary.

- Implementing consistent communication channels such as email updates or parent-teacher portals to share achievements and concerns promptly.

In addition to structured plans and meetings, informal interactions also contribute significantly to building trust and mutual respect among parents, teachers, and counselors. Celebrating successes together fosters a positive atmosphere that benefits not only the child but also strengthens the collaborative team's resolve to overcome challenges.

Ultimately, effective collaboration between parents, teachers, and school counselors is characterized by open dialogue, mutual respect, and a shared commitment to supporting the child's educational journey. By leveraging each other's strengths and expertise, this dynamic team can create an inclusive environment where every student has the opportunity to thrive academically and socially.

6.3 Creating an Inclusive Classroom Environment

The creation of an inclusive classroom environment is a critical aspect of modern education, aiming to accommodate the diverse needs of all students, including those with specific requirements such as OCD. This initiative goes beyond mere physical accessibility, delving into pedagogical strategies, social integration, and emotional support to foster a sense of belonging among all students. An inclusive classroom recognizes the individuality of each student and leverages this diversity to enrich the learning experience for everyone.

Inclusive education is not just about making adjustments for some but involves rethinking classroom dynamics and teaching methodologies to benefit all learners. It requires teachers to employ a variety of teaching styles that cater to a broad spectrum of learning preferences and abilities. For instance, incorporating visual aids, interactive activities, and technology can make lessons more engaging for students with different learning styles.

Another key element in creating an inclusive environment is promoting positive social interactions among students. This involves teaching empathy and respect, encouraging collaborative projects where students can learn from each other's strengths, and actively addressing any forms of bullying or exclusion. Teachers play a crucial role in modeling these behaviors and setting expectations for a supportive classroom culture.

- Implementing differentiated instruction techniques that tailor learning experiences according to individual student needs.

- Creating accessible learning materials that consider various disabilities and learning barriers.

- Fostering an open dialogue about diversity and inclusion within the classroom to promote understanding and acceptance.

Moreover, effective communication with parents and caregivers is vital in supporting the inclusive environment. Sharing insights about their child's progress, challenges, and achievements helps build trust and collaboration between home and school. This partnership ensures that strategies for inclusion extend beyond the classroom walls, creating a consistent support network for the child.

In conclusion, establishing an inclusive classroom environment is a multifaceted approach that demands commitment from educators, students, parents, and the wider school community. By embracing diversity as a strength rather than a challenge, schools can create nurturing spaces where every student has the opportunity to succeed academically and develop personally in a respectful and understanding atmosphere.

References:

- Florian, L. (2014). What counts as evidence of inclusive education? European Journal of Special Needs Education, 29(3), 286-294.

- Rose, D. H., & Meyer, A. (2002). Teaching every student in the digital age: Universal Design for Learning. Association for Supervision and Curriculum Development.

- Sapon-Shevin, M. (2007). Widening the circle: The power of inclusive classrooms. Beacon Press.

- Tompkins, G. E., & Hoskisson, K. (1995). Language arts: Content and teaching strategies. Merrill.

7

Addressing Common Challenges During Treatment

7.1 Handling Resistance to Treatment

Resistance to treatment in children with Obsessive-Compulsive Disorder (OCD) presents a significant challenge for caregivers, educators, and healthcare professionals. This resistance can manifest in various forms, from outright refusal to participate in therapy sessions to subtle avoidance of discussing feelings or complying with homework assignments designed to combat OCD symptoms. Understanding and addressing this resistance is crucial for the effective management of OCD in children.

The reasons behind treatment resistance are multifaceted and can include fear of change, discomfort with confronting obsessive thoughts or compulsive behaviors directly, and a lack of insight into the disorder itself. Children might also resist treatment due to feeling misunderstood by adults or fearing judgment from peers. It's essential for those involved in the child's care to approach resistance with empathy, patience, and a willingness to explore underlying concerns.

- Building Trust: Establishing a strong therapeutic alliance is foundational. Children need to feel safe and understood by their therapist or caregiver before they can begin to tackle the challenging work of managing their OCD symptoms.

- Educating About OCD: Providing age-appropriate information about OCD can demystify the condition for children and reduce any shame or fear associated with their experiences.

- Gradual Exposure: Starting with less anxiety-provoking situations before gradually moving on to more challenging ones can help ease children into the therapeutic process without overwhelming them.

- Involving the Child in Treatment Decisions: Giving children a say in their treatment can empower them and increase their engagement. This could mean allowing them to set small goals or choose between different therapeutic activities.

Moreover, incorporating elements of play or using metaphors that resonate with a child's interests can make therapy more relatable and less intimidating. Success stories or testimonials from other children who have successfully managed their OCD may also provide motivation and hope.

In conclusion, handling resistance requires a tailored approach that respects each child's unique needs and concerns. By fostering an environment of trust, understanding, and collaboration, caregivers and therapists can support children through their journey towards managing OCD effectively.

7.2 Dealing with Relapses and Setbacks

Relapses and setbacks are an inevitable part of the recovery journey for individuals dealing with Obsessive-Compulsive Disorder (OCD). Understanding how to navigate these challenges is crucial for both the individual and their support network, ensuring that progress towards managing OCD symptoms is not derailed. This section delves into strategies for effectively addressing relapses and setbacks, highlighting their role in the broader context of treatment and recovery.

Firstly, it's important to recognize that relapses do not signify failure but rather are a natural aspect of the healing process. They can serve as valuable learning opportunities, offering insights into triggers, stressors, or gaps in coping strategies. Acknowledging this perspective helps in maintaining motivation and resilience during difficult times.

- Early Identification: Recognizing early signs of a relapse can significantly impact its severity and duration. Individuals and caregivers should be educated on these signs to intervene promptly.

- Maintaining Routine: A structured routine involving therapy sessions, medication (if prescribed), and self-care activities can provide stability and reduce the likelihood of setbacks.

- Support Systems: Encouraging open communication within a supportive community or family structure ensures that individuals do not face setbacks alone. Peer support groups can also offer empathy, understanding, and practical advice from those with similar experiences.

- Cognitive Behavioral Techniques: Strengthening skills learned through Cognitive Behavioral Therapy (CBT), such as exposure response prevention (ERP) exercises or mindfulness practices, equips individuals to better manage obsessive thoughts or compulsive behaviors during challenging times.

In addition to these strategies, revisiting treatment plans regularly allows for adjustments based on current needs and challenges faced by the individual. This dynamic approach ensures that therapy remains relevant and effective over time. Furthermore, celebrating small victories along the way fosters a positive outlook and reinforces progress, even when facing setbacks.

In conclusion, dealing with relapses and setbacks requires a multifaceted approach that emphasizes early identification, routine maintenance, strong support systems, skill reinforcement through therapy techniques, and flexibility in treatment planning. By adopting these strategies within a framework of patience and compassion, individuals navigating OCD can continue making strides towards recovery despite occasional hurdles.

7.3 Maintaining Progress Over Time

Maintaining progress over time in the treatment of Obsessive-Compulsive Disorder (OCD) is a critical aspect that requires continuous effort and adaptation. After navigating through the initial challenges and learning to manage symptoms effectively, the long-term goal shifts towards sustaining these improvements and preventing relapse. This section explores strategies and insights into ensuring that progress made in managing OCD symptoms is maintained over time.

The journey of recovery from OCD is marked by its ups and downs. While dealing with relapses and setbacks forms one part of this journey, another equally important part is the sustained effort to maintain progress. This involves a combination of personal commitment, ongoing therapy, lifestyle adjustments, and support systems.

- Personal Commitment: The individual's dedication to continue practicing learned coping strategies plays a foundational role. This includes regular self-assessment to recognize potential triggers or signs of backsliding early on.

- Ongoing Therapy: Continuing engagement with therapeutic interventions such as Cognitive Behavioral Therapy (CBT) or Exposure Response Prevention (ERP) helps reinforce the skills necessary for managing OCD symptoms. Periodic sessions can provide an avenue for adjustment in techniques as life circumstances change.

- Lifestyle Adjustments: Incorporating healthy habits such as regular exercise, adequate sleep, and balanced nutrition supports overall well-being, which in turn can positively impact mental health. Stress management techniques like mindfulness or yoga can also be beneficial.

- Support Systems: Building and maintaining a strong network of support including family, friends, healthcare providers, and possibly peer support groups ensures that individuals have access to encouragement and guidance when needed.

Beyond these strategies, setting realistic goals and celebrating milestones are crucial for motivation. Recognizing even small achievements helps build confidence in one’s ability to manage their condition over the long term. Additionally, educating oneself about OCD continuously can empower individuals by making them feel more in control of their situation.

In conclusion, maintaining progress over time in managing OCD requires a multifaceted approach that emphasizes personal commitment to growth, ongoing therapeutic engagement, lifestyle modifications for overall well-being, and leveraging support networks. By focusing on these areas, individuals can enhance their resilience against potential setbacks and foster lasting improvement in their quality of life.

References:

- American Psychiatric Association. (2013). Diagnostic and Statistical Manual of Mental Disorders (5th ed.). Arlington, VA: American Psychiatric Publishing.

- International OCD Foundation. (n.d.). What is Cognitive Behavioral Therapy (CBT)? Retrieved from https://iocdf.org/about-ocd/ocd-treatment/cbt/

- National Institute of Mental Health. (2020). Obsessive-Compulsive Disorder: When Unwanted Thoughts or Repetitive Behaviors Take Over. Retrieved from https://www.nimh.nih.gov/health/topics/obsessive-compulsive-disorder-ocd

- Mind UK. (2019). Obsessive-compulsive disorder (OCD). Retrieved from https://www.mind.org.uk/information-support/types-of-mental-health-problems/obsessive-compulsive-disorder-ocd/.XkQ5iC2B1PY

8

Self-Care for Parents and Caregivers

8.1 Recognizing the Emotional Toll on Families

The journey of supporting a child with Obsessive-Compulsive Disorder (OCD) is fraught with challenges that extend beyond the child's individual struggles. For families, the emotional toll can be profound, affecting every member in unique and often unexpected ways. This section delves into the multifaceted impact of childhood OCD on families, highlighting the importance of acknowledging and addressing these emotional burdens to foster resilience and healing.

OCD does not exist in a vacuum; its ripples touch parents, siblings, and extended family members, altering dynamics and creating stressors that can strain even the strongest bonds. Parents may grapple with feelings of guilt, frustration, and helplessness as they navigate their child's condition. The relentless quest for effective treatments and interventions can be both time-consuming and emotionally draining, leaving little room for self-care or attention to other relationships within the family.

Siblings of children with OCD also face their own set of challenges. They may feel neglected or overshadowed by their sibling's needs, leading to feelings of resentment or jealousy. Additionally, witnessing their sibling's struggles with OCD symptoms can evoke feelings of confusion, fear, or sadness. It is crucial for parents and caregivers to recognize these emotional undercurrents and provide support tailored to each family member's needs.

- Open communication channels within the family to discuss feelings and concerns related to OCD.

- Seeking family therapy or support groups to navigate the emotional complexities together.

- Implementing self-care practices for all family members to mitigate stress and promote well-being.

The recognition of the emotional toll on families is a critical step towards building a supportive environment conducive to healing and growth. By addressing these challenges head-on, families can strengthen their bonds and become more resilient in the face of OCD. It underscores the necessity for comprehensive support systems that cater not only to the affected child but also to those around them who share in their journey.

8.2 Strategies for Parental Self-Care

The emotional and physical demands of caring for a child with Obsessive-Compulsive Disorder (OCD) can be overwhelming, making parental self-care an essential, yet often overlooked, aspect of family wellness. Recognizing the need for self-care is the first step towards sustaining one's health and well-being, enabling parents to provide the best possible support for their child. This section explores practical strategies that parents and caregivers can employ to maintain their own mental and physical health amidst the challenges of parenting a child with OCD.

Firstly, establishing a personal routine that includes regular breaks from caregiving duties is crucial. These breaks can be as simple as taking a short walk, reading a book, or engaging in any hobby that provides relaxation and joy. Itâ€™s important for parents to remember that taking time for themselves is not selfish but necessary for maintaining their capacity to care effectively.

- Implementing mindfulness practices such as meditation or yoga to reduce stress and enhance emotional equilibrium.

- Maintaining social connections with friends, family, or support groups who understand the unique challenges of raising a child with OCD.

- Seeking professional help when needed, whether it's counseling for emotional support or consulting healthcare providers for stress-related health issues.

Beyond individual activities, fostering open communication within the family unit is vital. Sharing feelings and experiences related to caregiving can help alleviate feelings of isolation or burden. Moreover, involving other family members in care responsibilities not only distributes the workload but also promotes understanding and empathy among siblings and partners.

Nutrition and physical activity are also key components of self-care. A balanced diet and regular exercise can significantly impact one’s mood and energy levels, improving overall resilience against stress. Lastly, ensuring adequate sleep is fundamental; sleep deprivation can exacerbate stress and diminish coping abilities.

In conclusion, adopting comprehensive self-care strategies enables parents to navigate the complexities of supporting a child with OCD more effectively. By prioritizing their own well-being through mindful practices, social support, professional assistance, balanced nutrition, physical activity, and sufficient rest, parents can strengthen their resilience and continue providing compassionate care without compromising their health.

8.3 Seeking Support from Communities and Groups

The journey of parenting or caregiving for a child with special needs, such as Obsessive-Compulsive Disorder (OCD), is one that need not be walked alone. The significance of seeking support from communities and groups cannot be overstated, as it offers a multifaceted approach to self-care that extends beyond the individual to encompass a broader network of shared experiences, resources, and emotional backing. This section delves into the various dimensions of community and group support, highlighting their pivotal role in enhancing parental resilience and well-being.

Firstly, the emotional solidarity found within support groups provides a unique space where parents can express their feelings, share their challenges, and celebrate successes without fear of judgment. These groups often facilitate a sense of belonging and understanding that can be hard to find elsewhere. Whether through formal support groups organized by mental health organizations or informal gatherings facilitated by community centers or online platforms, these connections can significantly mitigate feelings of isolation.

- Online forums and social media groups offer accessibility and anonymity for those who may not be ready for face-to-face interactions.

- Local community centers often host parent support meetings providing opportunities for real-life connection and networking.

- National and international organizations dedicated to OCD awareness have resources including helplines, workshops, and conferences that can empower parents with knowledge and strategies for care.

Beyond emotional support, communities often provide practical assistance in the form of shared resources. From recommendations for specialist care providers to navigating educational accommodations and legal rights, the collective wisdom of a community can be an invaluable asset. Moreover, advocacy groups play a crucial role in championing the needs of children with OCD at policy-making levels, thereby fostering environments more conducive to their growth and development.

In conclusion, integrating oneself into supportive communities offers manifold benefits that extend well beyond mere companionship. It equips parents with additional coping mechanisms through shared experiences, access to information and resources otherwise unknown or inaccessible, and collective advocacy efforts that pave the way for broader societal acceptance and understanding. Thus, seeking out these supports forms an essential pillar of comprehensive self-care for parents navigating the complexities of raising a child with OCD.

References:

- International OCD Foundation: Provides resources, support groups, and information on OCD for parents and caregivers (https://iocdf.org/).

- Anxiety and Depression Association of America (ADAA): Offers a searchable directory of support groups for those dealing with anxiety disorders, including OCD (https://adaa.org/).

- OCD-UK: A charity dedicated to helping those affected by OCD, offering advice, community forums, and advocacy information (https://www.ocduk.org/).

- Mental Health America: Provides a wide range of resources for mental health, including how to find support groups and community programs (https://mhanational.org/).

- The Mighty: An online social platform for people facing health challenges and disabilities to share their stories and connect with others (https://themighty.com/).

9

Real-Life Stories of Hope and Recovery

9.1 Case Studies of Children with OCD

The exploration of Obsessive-Compulsive Disorder (OCD) in children through case studies offers invaluable insights into the multifaceted nature of this condition, shedding light on the unique challenges and triumphs experienced by young individuals. These real-life stories not only humanize the clinical aspects of OCD but also provide a deeper understanding of the disorder's impact on daily life, family dynamics, and personal development.

One poignant case involves Alex, a 10-year-old whose obsession with cleanliness led to excessive handwashing. This ritual was driven by an overwhelming fear of germs and illness, causing significant distress and skin irritation. Through

Cognitive-Behavioral Therapy (CBT), Alex learned to confront these fears gradually, reducing the compulsion to wash hands excessively without eliminating necessary hygiene practices.

Sophia, an 8-year-old girl with OCD, struggled with intrusive thoughts that her family would be harmed if she didn't perform specific routines before bedtime. Her story illustrates the intense anxiety and responsibility children with OCD can feel, believing their actions directly influence unrelated outcomes. Sophia's treatment included Exposure and Response Prevention (ERP), helping her understand that these feared events remained unchanged regardless of her rituals, thereby lessening her compulsive behaviors over time.

Another case study focuses on Ethan, a 12-year-old who developed severe rituals around eating. His OCD manifested in needing to chew each bite a certain number of times before swallowing. This compulsion severely impacted his nutrition and social interactions. With a combination of medication management and therapy focused on gradual exposure to less structured eating habits, Ethan made significant progress towards normalcy in mealtime behaviors.

- Alex's journey underscores the importance of tailored therapeutic approaches that address both the physical and emotional aspects of OCD.

- Sophia's experience highlights how ERP can effectively reduce the power intrusive thoughts have over a child's actions.

- Ethan's recovery demonstrates that combining medication with behavioral therapy can be crucial for treating complex manifestations of OCD.

These case studies exemplify not just the struggles faced by children with OCD but also their capacity for resilience and recovery. They underscore the critical role of early intervention, specialized treatment plans, and supportive care networks in fostering positive outcomes. By sharing these stories, "OCD in Kids" aims to offer hope and practical guidance for families navigating similar challenges.

9.2 Lessons Learned from Families’ Journeys

The journey of families navigating the complexities of Obsessive-Compulsive Disorder (OCD) in a child offers profound insights into resilience, adaptation, and the transformative power of support and understanding. These narratives not only illuminate the challenges faced but also highlight the invaluable lessons learned through their experiences. By delving deeper into these stories, we uncover strategies and perspectives that can guide other families in similar situations.

One critical lesson is the importance of early recognition and intervention. Many families emphasize how recognizing the signs of OCD early on and seeking professional help made a significant difference in their child's progress. This early action facilitates a quicker adaptation to therapeutic strategies, potentially lessening the severity of symptoms over time.

Another key insight is the value of education and advocacy. Families who educated themselves about OCD were better equipped to advocate for their child's needs, whether in healthcare settings or educational environments. Understanding the disorder empowers parents to communicate more effectively with professionals and ensures that interventions are tailored to their child's specific challenges.

- Adapting family dynamics to support treatment goals is essential. Families learned that changes at home, such as establishing routines or modifying expectations around certain behaviors, could significantly reinforce therapeutic progress.

- Embracing flexibility in treatment approaches was another important lesson. What works for one child may not work for another, even within the same family. Being open to adjusting therapy techniques or trying new interventions was crucial for finding what best suited each child's unique needs.

- The power of community support cannot be overstated. Connecting with other families facing similar struggles provided a sense of belonging and understanding that was deeply comforting and informative.

In conclusion, these journeys underscore that while OCD presents significant challenges, there is also hope for recovery and growth. The shared experiences of these families highlight not just the necessity of personalized care but also the strength found in community, resilience in adversity, and the profound impact of informed advocacy. Through these stories, we gain not only insights into navigating OCD but also inspiration from each family's journey towards healing.

9.3 Celebrating Small Victories

The journey through Obsessive-Compulsive Disorder (OCD) with a child is fraught with challenges and setbacks, making it easy for families to become ensnared in a cycle of frustration and despair. However, amidst these trials, the practice of celebrating small victories emerges as a beacon of hope and progress. This section delves into the significance of acknowledging every step forward, no matter how minor it may seem, and explores how this approach can profoundly impact both the child's and the family's path to recovery.

Recognizing small victories is crucial because it shifts the focus from what is going wrong to what is going right. For a child struggling with OCD, each day can feel like a battleground. When parents and caregivers celebrate even the smallest successes, it not only boosts the child's morale but also reinforces their resilience. This positive reinforcement encourages more of the desired behavior, gradually leading to significant improvements over time.

Moreover, celebrating these moments helps in building a stronger bond between the child and their support system. It creates an environment of understanding and acceptance, where the child feels valued and supported regardless of their condition. This emotional foundation is critical for mental health recovery, providing the child with a sense of security that facilitates open communication about their struggles without fear of judgment or disappointment.

- Acknowledging efforts rather than outcomes emphasizes progress over perfection. This mindset helps in setting realistic expectations and fosters a growth-oriented approach to dealing with OCD.

- Incorporating creative ways to celebrate can make this practice more engaging for both children and adults. Whether itâ€™s a special meal, an extra half-hour of playtime, or a simple verbal affirmation, these celebrations can significantly enhance motivation.

- Documenting these victories can serve as a powerful reminder of how far the child has come on tougher days. Keeping a journal or creating a visual timeline can be therapeutic for both the child and family members.

In conclusion, celebrating small victories plays an indispensable role in navigating OCD with hope and positivity. It teaches families that while OCD is part of their lives, it does not define them or their capacity for joy and achievement. By cherishing each step forward, families cultivate an atmosphere where growth is celebrated, resilience is built, and recovery becomes an attainable goal marked by countless victories along the way.

References:

- March, J.S., & Benton, C.M. (2007). Treating Your OCD with Exposure and Response (Ritual) Prevention Therapy: Workbook. Oxford University Press. This workbook provides practical guidance for individuals and families dealing with OCD, emphasizing the importance of celebrating progress.

- Foa, E.B., Yadin, E., & Lichner, T.K. (2012). Exposure and Response (Ritual) Prevention for Obsessive-Compulsive Disorder: Therapist Guide. Oxford University Press. A comprehensive guide for therapists that underscores the significance of acknowledging small achievements in the treatment of OCD.

- Hershfield, J., & Corboy, T. (2013). The Mindfulness Workbook for OCD: A Guide to Overcoming Obsessions and Compulsions Using Mindfulness and Cognitive Behavioral Therapy. New Harbinger Publications. This workbook introduces mindfulness as a tool for managing OCD and highlights the value of celebrating every victory along the journey.

10

Beyond Treatment - Thriving with OCD

10.1 Long-Term Management Strategies

The journey of managing OCD, especially in children, is often a long-term commitment that extends beyond initial treatment phases. Understanding and implementing effective long-term management strategies are crucial for helping children with OCD not just survive but thrive in their daily lives. These strategies serve as the foundation for building resilience against the disorder's challenges, ensuring that children can lead fulfilling lives despite their condition.

One of the core components of long-term management involves maintaining a consistent routine around therapy and medication adherence. For many families, navigating the complexities of medication schedules and therapy sessions can be daunting. However, consistency is key to managing symptoms effectively over time. It's also important for caregivers to stay informed about any new developments in OCD treatments or therapies that might benefit their child.

In addition to these strategies, fostering open communication about OCD within the family encourages an environment where children feel safe to express their feelings and struggles without fear of judgment. This openness helps demystify the disorder and promotes a healthier emotional climate at home.

Ultimately, long-term management of OCD in children requires patience, persistence, and adaptability from everyone involved. By embracing these strategies, families can navigate the ups and downs of OCD together, supporting their child's journey towards resilience and empowerment.

- Engagement in regular therapeutic activities: Whether it's continuing with cognitive-behavioral therapy (CBT) sessions or participating in support groups, staying engaged with therapeutic activities helps reinforce coping mechanisms and provides ongoing support.

- Educational advocacy: Ensuring that children receive the necessary accommodations at school is vital for their academic success and self-esteem. This may include working closely with educators to implement individualized education plans (IEPs) or 504 plans tailored to the child's needs.

- Mindfulness and stress reduction techniques: Teaching children mindfulness exercises can empower them to manage anxiety more effectively. Techniques such as deep breathing, meditation, or yoga can be beneficial tools for reducing stress and improving overall well-being.

- Building a supportive community: Cultivating a network of support among family members, friends, teachers, and healthcare providers creates a safety net for both the child and caregivers. This community can offer encouragement, understanding, and practical help when needed.

10.2 Preparing for Adolescence and Adulthood

The transition from childhood into adolescence and adulthood presents unique challenges and opportunities for individuals with OCD. This period is marked by significant physical, emotional, and social changes that can influence the course of the disorder. Preparing for these life stages involves a multifaceted approach that builds on the foundation of long-term management strategies while introducing new concepts tailored to the evolving needs of young people.

One critical aspect of preparation involves education about the nature of OCD and its potential fluctuations over time. Adolescents should be equipped with knowledge about how stressors related to puberty, social relationships, academic pressures, and future planning can impact their symptoms. Empowering them with this understanding fosters resilience, enabling them to anticipate and manage possible exacerbations or new manifestations of their OCD.

- Enhancing self-advocacy skills: As children mature, they take on greater responsibility for their health care decisions. Teaching adolescents to advocate for themselves in medical settings, educational institutions, and social contexts ensures they can secure necessary accommodations and support.

- Transitioning care: Moving from pediatric to adult health care services is a pivotal step. This process should be navigated thoughtfully, ensuring continuity of care and that the chosen health care professionals are well-versed in treating OCD in adults.

- Developing independence: Encouraging age-appropriate independence in daily living, decision-making, and problem-solving helps young adults build confidence in their ability to manage life's challenges without being overly reliant on others.

- Maintaining social connections: Fostering strong relationships with peers who provide understanding and support is crucial during this time when isolation can exacerbate OCD symptoms.

Beyond these specific strategies, it's essential to continue promoting general well-being through healthy lifestyle choices such as regular exercise, adequate sleep, balanced nutrition, and engaging in hobbies or activities that bring joy. These practices contribute to overall mental health resilience.

In conclusion, preparing adolescents with OCD for adulthood requires a comprehensive approach that addresses their changing needs while reinforcing the coping strategies developed during childhood. By doing so, individuals are better positioned to navigate the complexities of adult life with confidence and competence despite the challenges posed by OCD.

10.3 Empowering Children to Lead Fulfilling Lives

The journey from childhood through adolescence into adulthood is a pivotal phase for individuals with OCD, laden with both challenges and opportunities for growth. Empowering children to lead fulfilling lives despite their disorder involves a comprehensive strategy that not only addresses the symptoms of OCD but also nurtures their overall development and well-being. This section delves into the multifaceted approach required to equip children with the tools they need to thrive.

Understanding the unique needs of children with OCD is crucial in fostering an environment where they can flourish. This includes recognizing the importance of early intervention and tailored support systems that cater to their emotional, social, and educational needs. By creating a supportive framework around these young individuals, caregivers and professionals can significantly influence their trajectory towards leading rewarding lives.

- Building resilience through education: Educating children about their condition empowers them with knowledge and demystifies their experiences. This foundational understanding enables them to recognize symptoms, understand treatment options, and actively participate in their care plan.

- Encouraging social engagement: Developing strong social connections is vital for emotional support and reducing feelings of isolation often associated with OCD. Activities that promote interaction with peers can enhance self-esteem and provide a sense of belonging.

- Promoting independence: Gradually introducing responsibilities and decision-making opportunities helps children gain confidence in their abilities. Encouraging problem-solving skills and autonomy prepares them for future challenges while ensuring they feel capable of managing aspects of their disorder independently.

- Nurturing interests and talents: Engaging in hobbies or activities that spark joy can be therapeutic for children with OCD. These pursuits offer an outlet for creativity, reduce stress, and contribute to a positive self-image.

In conclusion, empowering children with OCD to lead fulfilling lives requires a holistic approach that goes beyond managing symptoms. It involves nurturing their resilience, fostering meaningful connections, promoting independence, and encouraging personal interests. By addressing these areas comprehensively, caregivers can help pave the way for these young individuals to achieve not just stability but genuine happiness and success in life.

References:

- American Psychiatric Association. (2013). Diagnostic and statistical manual of mental disorders (5th ed.). Arlington, VA: American Psychiatric Publishing.

- March, J.S., & Benton, C.M. (2007). The role of family and peer relationships in the treatment of pediatric obsessive-compulsive disorder. Clinical Child and Family Psychology Review, 10(4), 298-308.

- Piacentini, J., Bergman, R.L., Keller, M., & McCracken, J. (2003). Functional impairment in children and adolescents with obsessive-compulsive disorder. Journal of Child and Adolescent Psychopharmacology, 13(Suppl 1), S61-S69.

- Storch, E.A., Murphy, T.K., Geffken, G.R., Sajid, M., & Goodman, W.K. (2004). Psychosocial interventions for children and adolescents with obsessive-compulsive disorder: A review. Journal of Pediatric Psychology, 29(2), 129-139.

11

Resources for Further Support

1.1 Recommended Reading List

The importance of a curated reading list cannot be overstated, especially when it comes to understanding and managing Obsessive Compulsive Disorder (OCD) in children. "OCD in Kids: Obsessive Compulsive Disorder In Children Survival Guide" serves as an essential starting point for anyone looking to deepen their comprehension of this complex condition. However, expanding one's knowledge through additional resources can provide a more rounded perspective and offer various approaches to support affected children effectively.

Building upon the foundation laid by the survival guide, the recommended reading list includes works that delve into different aspects of OCD, from clinical research and treatment methodologies to personal narratives that offer insight into the lived experiences of individuals with OCD. This multifaceted approach ensures that parents, caregivers, educators, and even older children themselves can find valuable information tailored to their specific needs or interests.

- "Freeing Your Child from Obsessive-Compulsive Disorder" by Tamar E. Chansky - A book that provides a step-by-step program for helping children overcome OCD with practical strategies.

- "Talking Back to OCD" by John S. March - Offers guidance on how parents can support their child through Cognitive Behavioral Therapy (CBT) techniques.

- "Up and Down the Worry Hill" by Aureen Pinto Wagner - A children's book that explains OCD in a way that is accessible and relatable for young readers.

- "The OCD Workbook for Kids" by Anthony C. Puliafico and Joanna A. Robin - Provides exercises and activities designed to help children manage their OCD symptoms.

Including these titles alongside "OCD in Kids" enriches the pool of resources available to those seeking to understand or combat OCD in children. Each book contributes unique insights into effective treatment options, coping mechanisms, and supportive practices that can make a significant difference in the lives of affected families. By exploring these varied perspectives, readers are better equipped to create a nurturing environment where children with OCD can thrive.

This comprehensive exploration not only broadens awareness but also empowers readers with an arsenal of tools and strategies for dealing with OCD. The journey through understanding and managing this condition is made less daunting with such resources at one's disposal, highlighting the power of informed support and compassionate intervention.

11.2 Professional Organizations and Online Platforms

The landscape of support for individuals dealing with Obsessive Compulsive Disorder (OCD), especially in children, has been significantly enriched by the advent of professional organizations and online platforms. These entities not only provide a wealth of resources tailored to various needs but also foster communities where shared experiences and strategies can be exchanged. This section delves into the pivotal role these organizations and platforms play in offering support, advancing research, and promoting awareness about OCD.

Professional organizations dedicated to OCD have been instrumental in bridging the gap between clinical research and practical support for families. They offer a range of services from educational materials, professional directories to find specialized care, to funding research aimed at better understanding and treating OCD. Organizations such as the International OCD Foundation (IOCDF) exemplify this by hosting annual conferences that bring together individuals with OCD, their families, and professionals in the field to share knowledge and experiences.

Online platforms complement these efforts by providing accessible forums for discussion, peer support groups, and repositories of articles and tools related to OCD management. Websites like BeyondOCD.org offer guides on recognizing symptoms, understanding treatment options, and tips for parents on supporting their children through their journey with OCD. Similarly, social media groups and online forums have become invaluable spaces for individuals affected by OCD to connect with others facing similar challenges, fostering a sense of community and mutual support that can be particularly empowering.

- Webinars and Workshops: Many professional organizations host online events that allow for real-time interaction with experts in the field.

- Educational Resources: Access to a wide array of articles, videos, and interactive tools designed to educate about OCD.

- Support Networks: Online platforms often facilitate connections between individuals seeking peer support or advice from professionals.

In conclusion, professional organizations and online platforms play a critical role in providing comprehensive support systems for those impacted by OCD. By leveraging these resources, individuals can gain insights into effective treatment methodologies, connect with specialists focused on pediatric OCD care, and find solace in communities that understand their unique challenges. The synergy between these entities enhances the overall ecosystem of support available, making it an indispensable aspect of managing OCD in children.

11.3 Finding Local Support Groups

Finding local support groups is a crucial step for individuals and families navigating the complexities of Obsessive Compulsive Disorder (OCD), particularly when it comes to creating a supportive community environment. These groups offer a unique platform where experiences, coping strategies, and personal insights can be shared among those who truly understand the challenges faced by someone with OCD. This section explores the importance of local support groups in providing emotional solace and practical advice, expanding upon the foundational role that professional organizations and online platforms play in the broader ecosystem of OCD support.

Local support groups serve as an invaluable resource for direct, face-to-face interaction, which can be especially comforting. The sense of belonging and understanding that comes from meeting others facing similar struggles cannot be understated. These groups often organize regular meetings, workshops, and social events that not only help reduce feelings of isolation but also empower members with knowledge about managing OCD. Furthermore, local support groups can provide recommendations for therapists, clinics, and other resources within the community that are specialized in treating OCD.

- Community Connections: Engaging with a local support group helps build a network of peers who understand what it means to live with OCD. This network can become a powerful tool for both newly diagnosed individuals and those who have been managing their condition over time.

- Educational Opportunities: Many local groups invite experts to speak on various aspects of OCD, including treatment options, latest research findings, and strategies for coping with daily challenges.

- Mutual Support: Sharing personal stories and solutions offers mutual encouragement and fosters an environment where members can learn from each other's experiences.

To find local support groups, individuals can start by consulting professionals involved in their care or by reaching out to national or international OCD organizations which often maintain directories of local chapters. Additionally, exploring community bulletin boardsâ€"both physical ones in libraries or community centers and digital ones on social media or dedicated websitesâ€"can uncover nearby meetings. It's important to remember that while finding the right group may take time, the benefits of connecting with others who understand firsthand the journey through OCD are immeasurable.

In conclusion, while professional organizations and online platforms offer broad-based support and information accessible from anywhere, local support groups add a deeply personal dimension to the spectrum of available resources. They embody the principle that while each personâ€™s journey with OCD is unique, no one has to navigate it alone. The collective wisdom found in these communities enriches individual lives by offering hope, understanding, and tangible assistance on the path towards managing OCD more effectively.

References:

- International OCD Foundation: Provides a comprehensive directory of local support groups for individuals and families dealing with OCD. Visit iocdf.org for more information.

- Anxiety and Depression Association of America (ADAA): Offers resources and tools to find local support groups focusing on anxiety, depression, and OCD. Check out their website at adaa.org.

- Mental Health America: A leading community-based nonprofit dedicated to addressing the needs of those living with mental illness and promoting overall mental health. Their site mhanational.org includes resources for finding support groups.

- OCD-UK: A charity focused on helping those affected by OCD. They provide information on local support groups in the UK. Visit their website at ocduk.org.

12

Embracing the Journey Ahead

12.1 Reflecting on Growth and Resilience

The journey of managing Obsessive Compulsive Disorder (OCD) in children is both challenging and enlightening for families, educators, and healthcare professionals involved. Reflecting on growth and resilience becomes a pivotal aspect of this journey, offering insights into the adaptive capabilities that both children with OCD and their support networks develop over time. This reflection not only acknowledges the hurdles overcome but also celebrates the strength found in adversity.

Growth in this context refers to the personal development experienced by children as they learn to navigate their world with OCD. It encompasses acquiring new coping strategies, achieving milestones in therapy, and gradually taking control over the symptoms that once seemed insurmountable. For parents and caregivers, growth might manifest as an increased understanding of OCD, enhanced empathy towards their child’s struggles, and the ability to provide unwavering support through ups and downs.

Resilience shines through as families encounter setbacks or when progress seems slow. It is found in the determination to keep moving forward despite occasional relapses or when treatment does not produce immediate results. Children show resilience when they apply therapeutic techniques to manage their symptoms or when they bravely face situations that trigger their OCD. Similarly, resilience is evident in parents who tirelessly advocate for their child’s needs, whether seeking appropriate educational accommodations or ensuring consistent access to effective treatments.

In reflecting on growth and resilience, it becomes clear that overcoming the challenges posed by childhood OCD is not solely about reducing symptoms but also about fostering an environment where children can thrive despite them. This holistic approach emphasizes the importance of nurturing emotional well-being alongside pursuing clinical interventions. Ultimately, reflecting on these aspects encourages a deeper appreciation for the journey itselfâ€"a path marked by learning, adaptation, and profound strength.

- Recognizing small victories: Celebrating even minor improvements can boost morale and encourage continued effort towards managing OCD.

- Building a supportive community: Finding or creating networks with other families navigating similar challenges can provide invaluable emotional support and practical advice.

- Maintaining hope: Keeping a hopeful outlook is crucial for sustaining motivation across all stages of dealing with OCD.

12.2 The Importance of Continued Education

The journey of managing Obsessive Compulsive Disorder (OCD) in children is a multifaceted process that extends beyond initial diagnosis and treatment. It encompasses a continuous learning curve for children, families, educators, and healthcare professionals alike. The importance of continued education in this context cannot be overstated, as it plays a crucial role in adapting to the evolving nature of OCD and its impact on the childâ€™s life.

Continued education serves several key purposes in the management of childhood OCD. Firstly, it ensures that all parties involved are up-to-date with the latest research findings and treatment methodologies. The field of mental health is rapidly advancing, and new insights can significantly alter approaches to care. For healthcare professionals, staying informed about recent studies or innovative therapeutic techniques enhances their ability to provide effective treatment. For families and educators, understanding these advancements can lead to more supportive environments for the child both at home and in school.

Moreover, continued education fosters an environment of empathy and understanding by debunking myths and reducing stigma associated with OCD. Knowledge dispels fear; as parents, teachers, and peers learn more about what OCD entails, their capacity for compassion grows. This shift not only benefits the emotional well-being of the child but also promotes inclusivity within communities.

- Engaging with support groups: These forums can be invaluable sources of information, shared experiences, and practical advice.

- Participating in workshops and seminars: Such events often feature experts in the field who provide deeper insights into managing OCD.

- Utilizing online resources: Websites, webinars, and online courses offer flexible learning opportunities for those seeking to expand their knowledge.

In essence, continued education is a dynamic component of managing childhood OCD that empowers all involved parties to contribute positively to the child's development and well-being. It encourages proactive engagement with new information and strategies that can facilitate better outcomes over time. By embracing continued education as a cornerstone of OCD management, families can navigate the complexities of the disorder with greater confidence and resilience.

12.3 Fostering a Future of Hope

In the journey of managing Obsessive Compulsive Disorder (OCD) in children, fostering a future of hope is an essential step that follows naturally from the foundation laid by continued education. This phase is about building upon the knowledge and understanding gained to create an environment where children feel empowered and optimistic about their futures. It involves not just the children affected by OCD but also their families, educators, and healthcare providers working collaboratively towards a common goal.

Hope is a powerful motivator. It encourages resilience in the face of challenges and fosters a belief in positive outcomes. For children with OCD, having hope means believing that they can lead fulfilling lives despite their disorder. This belief is crucial for their mental health and overall well-being. It can reduce feelings of isolation or despair, making it easier for them to engage with treatment and support systems.

To foster this sense of hope, several strategies can be employed:

- Highlighting success stories: Sharing narratives of individuals who have successfully managed their OCD can inspire children and their families. These stories provide tangible examples of what can be achieved with perseverance and support.

- Setting achievable goals: Working with children to set realistic, short-term goals gives them a sense of accomplishment and progress. These goals should be tailored to the individual's capabilities and interests, reinforcing their confidence and self-esteem.

- Promoting positive relationships: Encouraging strong connections with peers, family members, and mentors provides emotional support that is critical for fostering hope. Positive relationships offer encouragement and understanding, which are vital during difficult periods.

- Integrating mindfulness practices: Techniques such as meditation or yoga can help children manage anxiety symptoms associated with OCD. By learning to live in the moment, they may gain a more hopeful perspective on life.

Fostering a future of hope requires patience, dedication, and continuous effort from everyone involved in the child's care network. It's about creating an ecosystem that nurtures optimism through every interaction and experience. By prioritizing hope alongside education and treatment strategies, we pave the way for children with OCD to envision brighter futures filled with possibilities.

References:

- American Psychiatric Association. (2013). Diagnostic and Statistical Manual of Mental Disorders (5th ed.). Arlington, VA: American Psychiatric Publishing.

- March, J.S., & Benton, C.M. (2007). Treating OCD in Children and Adolescents: A Cognitive-Behavioral Approach. New York, NY: Guilford Press.

- Piacentini, J., & Langley, A.K. (2004). Cognitive-behavioral therapy for children who have obsessive-compulsive disorder. Journal of Clinical Psychology, 60(11), 1181-1194.

- Selles, R.R., & Storch, E.A. (2019). Mindfulness-Based Cognitive Therapy for Children with Obsessive-Compulsive Disorder: An Open Trial. Journal of Child and Adolescent Psychopharmacology, 29(6), 449-456.

"OCD in Kids: Obsessive Compulsive Disorder In Children Survival Guide" is a comprehensive resource aimed at assisting parents, caregivers, and educators in understanding and managing obsessive-compulsive disorder (OCD) in children. This non-fiction book breaks down the complexities of OCD into understandable segments, shedding light on a condition that affects millions of children globally with a range of perplexing symptoms. The guide is enriched with insights from psychologists, pediatricians, and therapists specializing in childhood OCD, offering a blend of empathy and practical strategies for those supporting affected children.

The book starts by clarifying what OCD is, distinguishing it from the usual worries or rituals seen in child development. It uses real-life stories and case studies to illustrate the varied manifestations of OCD in children, aiming to foster empathy and comprehension among readers. Central to the guide is its actionable advice on recognizing early signs of OCD, understanding triggers, navigating diagnosis with patience, and creating a supportive environment for open communication.

Significantly, the book explores various treatment options tailored for children, including cognitive-behavioral therapy (CBT), medication management tips, and holistic approaches like mindfulness exercises. It also tackles challenges families might face during treatment and offers solutions to maintain progress and prevent relapses. Additionally, it provides self-care strategies for parents and caregivers to remain resilient sources of support.

Furthermore, "OCD in Kids" extends its utility to educational settings by advising on advocating for accommodations that support academic success and detailing how teachers can foster inclusive environments. Overall, this survival guide serves as an essential companion for anyone involved in the life of a child with OCD, offering hope, wisdom, and practical support through every step of their journey.